Real Estate Investing
The Creative Way

By John R Mitchell

Contents

Chapter 2: The Basics

Section 1. Deeds

Subsection 1. General Warranty Deeds

Subsection 2. Special Warranty Deeds

Subsection 3. Quitclaim Deeds

Section 2. Real Estate Attorneys

Subsection 1.

Limited Liability

Companies + Series

Subsection 2.

Partnerships

Subsection 3.

Trusts

Section 2. Three

Model

Foreword

I would first like to take this opportunity to thank my personal Mentor, who has helped to teach and shape me into the kick ass author, and successful business man that I am today. I would also like to thank the teachers who have imbued me with the knowledge that I can now share with those around me. Most importantly, I would like to thank you, my dear reader. It is only because of your will to become better than you were yesterday, that I can sit, and write this guidebook to help you along your journey.

In chapter one, you will learn the differences between traditional and creative real estate investments. You will learn the thought process, and state of mind you should be in to begin your journey. Most importantly, you will learn why creative real estate is the future of real estate investing, as well as the short window we find ourselves in to make big moves. Much like the oil booms, and gold rushes of old, real estate is currently suffering through a sort of restructuring, and this book will best position you to take full advantage of these opportunities.

In chapter two, you will learn all you need to know about deeds. The differences between deeds and how to best choose a deed for your current situation. You will also have an opportunity to read about Real Estate Attorneys, and why you should consider finding one to work with. There will also be a short section on title companies, and the services they provide. Lastly, you will delve into the subject of mortgages.

In chapter three, you will take a quick crash course in networking and online marketing. These two concepts will form the base for your business, and provide you with unlimited deals to structure. You will also be introduced to the world of hard-money lending. Being able to network between buyers, suppliers, and lenders, will be a key concept for this chapter.

Chapter four will be a little denser. You will have the opportunity to delve into contract flipping. This is the commonly the first way to dip your toes into creative investing. Then you will read about flipping houses, which is a little more intensive, but will lead to more profits. Then you will read a bonus section, which describes a unique hybrid of traditional, and creative investing. For those of you who might be interested in such a thing.

The last chapter, chapter five, will be all about business entities, as well as structuring your business. There will be a section on LLCs, plus the new Series LLC, Partnerships, and Trusts. All of these are common business entities seen in the world of real estate investing. The last section of the chapter, will cover three different business models. These are models that have been devised by yours truly, and will help to jump start your carrier in creative real estate!

Chapter 1

Traditional VS Creative

Section 1

Traditional Real Estate

When you think of real estate investing you are really thinking of what this author likes to refer to as "Traditional Real Estate". Tradition is defined as customs or beliefs transferred from generation to generation. Tradition is the reason there is a Queen in England that wears diamond encrusted tiaras, and makes visiting the country feel magical, and unique. Tradition is also the reason for the Salem Witch Trials, but I digress.

For many generations if you wanted to become a real estate investor you had to have large stashes of capital laying around, either from old family money, or a very successful business. Then you might go out into the world, and find some properties that tickle your fancy, possibly do a little due diligence, make an application to a bank, throw down 20% and get yourself a nifty mortgage.

At this point you had a few options. First, you could rent out the property and structure the rent payments in such a way as to "pass through"[1] you and pay your mortgage with a little left over in your pocket every month. Of course, if you're wise at managing your income you'll deposit a portion of the money you receive every month in a savings account to build up a reserve should anything break on the property and you need to repair it. If not, you risk being "cash poor"[2], and this can lead you to make bad choices that might land

---

[1] Literally, the money moves through your accounts.
[2] Having plenty of assets, but not enough cash on hand.

you in hot water! Remember, it's very easy to get sued as a landlord!

Your second option involves a little more legwork, but has a nice payoff. You attain a property as described above, but instead of renting the property, you simply find someone with deep pockets willing to buy the property. Ideally, the purchase price should be sufficient to cover the mortgage amount, plus any expenses incurred and time spent putting the deal together. This method has the benefit of not becoming a landlord, which carries risk, but does limit the market of people you can sell to. Still, not a bad payday for an honest day's work!

If you're a little more aggressive with your investing, there is still a third option that might interest you. In this instance, you find a property you want to purchase and do your due diligence, but you finance it yourself. You simply buy the property with your own money. Now you can choose to rent the property out, and squeeze a little more money out of the rent payments every month. You could also choose to become the lender, and write your own mortgage to whoever buys the property. Once you have the mortgage, you can cash in every month on the payments, or simply sell the mortgage to somebody else, although this would require you deduct a percentage off the top.

Of course, that third options carries a lot of inherent risks. If you finance yourself, you risk taking a huge hit if the property turns out to have major issues, or if the market takes a big dip. Not to mention that being a landlord carries a lot of risks naturally, refer back to this author's comment about the ease with which one gets sued.

For a long time, generations even, these examples have been the backbone of real estate investing. It's a rigid system filled with technicalities and speed bumps. If you had huge cash reserves, at least that greased the wheels. Banks are more willing to provide you credit to mortgage multiple properties at once, or you could afford to finance a portfolio yourself. Even so, having money doesn't guarantee success in traditional real estate. If you're bad at managing your cash flow, or you get sued a lot, or if the market takes a turn for the worse, and you're left with bad investments, you could be facing bankruptcy quicker than you think.

There have been plenty of people who lost a

fortune to any of the issues raised above. Therein lies the problem with traditional real estate, it's an old institution that lacks flexibility!

That brings us, dear reader, to the point I've been trying to make in this section. If you want to succeed in real estate investing, you have to cast off the shackles of tradition, you must learn to become flexible and most importantly, how to think outside the box. In the subsequent chapters and sections of this book, we will go on a journey through what this author likes to refer to as "Creative Real Estate".

You will learn the basics of real estate which will form a solid foundation of knowledge. You will explore new concepts that will allow you to hit the road running, and start making investments with little or no money down. Most importantly, this book will teach you to think in a new way, which will lead to new concepts that may someday earn you a fortune. As this author's Mentor always says, "You never know what little piece of information, what little insignificant detail, will grow into a million dollar idea."

Section 2

Creative Real Estate

If you've made it this far into the book, then you deserve a pat on the back! Seriously, if you're still reading that implies that you have an open mind for new ideas, and a tenacity to try out new concepts. Most people would not even consider reading a book on real estate investing. They might say to themselves, "I don't have the time or money!", or "I could never learn to do that!". So, you deserve some recognition for picking up this book and being willing to learn something new.

With that being said, you might be wondering what "Creative Real Estate" is all about. The first thing to address is that traditionally (there's that word again), creative real estate has been looked upon with a little disdain. There's been a stigma attached to creative real estate, and people assume that a creative investor is unscrupulous. They might think that you, my dear reader, are trying to take the easy way and make some quick money off the backs of the working poor. That is simply not true!

Creative Real Estate, or creative investing for short, is just the act of taking traditional, established concepts about real estate, and introducing new methods that others simply haven't thought of, or have the fortitude to attempt. You're not trying to re-invent the wheel, you're simply learning new ways to use it. Just because you're making no-money down deals, or structuring deals in ways that aren't common, does not mean you're a shady character. You're only being a shrewd business person, who is willing to step outside the comfort zone, and take action on opportunities that present themselves.

Most importantly, being a creative investor means attaining a new mindset. When you think of creative investing, you should think of a liaison. That is essentially what you will become. A successful creative investor will learn to source good real estate deals, as well as eager buyers, and will structure deals that benefit all of the parties involved. There's a lot of legwork involved, and you will have to learn how to market yourself, and network with the right people. In the end, these will become your most powerful tools.

In later chapters you will study in more

detail what are the types of deals you will be putting together, but for now, let's cover some methods in a broad stroke. Unlike traditional real estate, creative real estate investors don't follow the standard approach to making deals. Were in traditional investing, you might contact real estate agents, or skim through the classifieds to source good properties, in creative investing, we network with executives and portfolio managers for national servicing companies. A servicing company, my dear reader, is a business that specializes in managing and selling properties for banks. Banks will often times attain large numbers of properties they can't resell, either through foreclosures, auctions, etc.

You might remember that back in 2008, there was a meltdown in real estate due to the incredibly high number of bad mortgages? That meltdown resulted in millions of defaults that has led to banks, and other financial institutions, to repossess all of those properties with no immediate way of liquidating them. Banks are not geared toward sales, they are lending institutions. That is why many of those banks have brokered deals with servicing companies to manage and sell the properties for them. Here is where another problem arises, these servicing companies are also not very good at selling!

This is where the window of opportunity mentioned earlier is opened. There are millions of properties that are owned by banks and other institutions, these banks aren't interested in becoming sellers, and they can't very well dump all of those properties into the open market at once without imploding it.

The banks hire servicing companies and feed them a certain number of properties every month, in hopes that the properties can be liquidated, and the banks can mitigate their loses, however, these servicing companies don't have the means, or desire, to deal with "mom & pop"[3] investors. That is where you, dear reader, will come into play, and fill the gap that otherwise won't be filled.

Your job is simply to connect with the portfolio managers at these servicing companies, and source a portion of their properties, then you can turn around, and structure deals with the "mom & pop" buyers you found, which the portfolio managers cannot, and will not deal with. There are two powerful methods that you can use to make these deals happen. The first one is the

---

[3] Small time, maybe only one, or two investors.

simplest, and quickest, it's called "Flipping the Contract"[4], the second is more intensive, but also offers more reward, it's knowns as "Flipping the House"[5]. Before we cover these two methods, and turn you into a master at networking, and marketing, let us begin with the basics of real estate!

---

[4] Refer to section 1 of chapter 4.
[5] Refer to section 2 of chapter 4.

Chapter 2

The Basics

Section 1

Deeds

If you are going to learn the basics of real estate, it is imperative that we begin with the most fundamentally important document to real estate investing, and that would be the deed. Deeds are written documents that convey the legal and equitable title of real property. In layman's terms, deeds are the "title"[6] to the property being bought.

Deeds are an extremely important subject for real estate investors, however, they are also an extremely vast, and complex subject to cover. There is NO standard format for a deed. Usually deeds are written by in-house lawyers working for title companies, and they are not

---

[6] Imagine a car title, a piece of paper that shows ownership.

interested in providing a deed that is particularly beneficial to the buyer or seller, and those are as close to standard as you might get. There are many types of deeds in use all across the U.S., and there are many, many, *many* changes that can be made to deeds to better suit a party. Of course, deeds are best left to real estate lawyers with experience writing them, but there is no reason you should not know the basics! Having said all of that, I will write this section shorter than most and only cover the bare bones of a deed in a bullet point style. Then, I will write, just for you my dear reader, another three sections, detailing the three most common deeds found today; General Warranty Deeds, Special Warranty Deeds, and Quitclaim Deeds. Here are six points to remember when dealing with deeds:

1. Deeds don't have to be registered in the real property records, in the county where the property resides, however, registering a deed is a great way to keep the chain of title ownership intact, and is in fact greatly encouraged.

2. Deeds need only be signed by the seller, in this instance known formally as the "grantor"[7], but could also be signed by the buyer, known as the "grantee"[8]. This usually happens when the grantee has an obligation to fulfill some duty after receiving the deed, so signing stands as formal notice, and the clock starts ticking.

3. In community property states, and

---

[7] Term associated with deeds. The grantor is the person conveying ownership.

[8] Term associated with deeds. The grantee is the person receiving ownership.

sometimes in non-community property states, deeds will outline the marriage status of both the grantee and grantor. If a deed does not have this information, title companies will ask for an affidavit of marriage before issuing title insurance.

4. Deeds are not required to state the amount the property was sold for, they could have no amount listed, or an amount stated as "$100 and other considerations", or the entire amount.

5. Deeds are encouraged to be very specific about the property mentioned, this can be done with "metes and bounds" or "lot and block". If an investor handles many deeds at once, it is fine to include the street address in a deed, this is a practical way to not confuse which deed goes to what property.

6. Deeds can be heavily modified to be advantageous for the grantor or grantee. It all depends on the lawyer who wrote the deed up.

Well, there you have it! A quick and dirty run down on deeds. Again, this is not by any means an exhaustive study in deeds. However, you will go on to learn about three common deeds in the following sections. Be sure to have a solid understanding of these facts, as well as the sections to follow. This information will give you a solid foundation of knowledge that most investors are lacking, which can lead to more self-confidence when negotiating, and ultimately, better deals!

Subsection 1

General Warranty Deeds

General Warranty Deeds are, by far, the most pervasive in the residential real estate market. They are a very old instrument, which has been around long enough to be considered the traditional format for deeds. While the name may seem intimidating at first, they are a fairly simple beast to understand. Let's break it down!

As the name would imply, these deeds imply general warranties, or promises, that bind the Grantor, to defend the Grantee, and rectify any defects in title, that originate from the Grantor's ownership all the way back to the provenance of the property. It becomes easier to visualize the concept, when you study and understand the four warranties, or covenants, that come standard in these deeds. Let's quickly outline these covenants:

1. Covenant of Seisin: A promise by the Grantor, of true ownership, as well as the quality of the property represented during negotiations.

2. Covenant of the Right to Convey: A promise by the Grantor, that the Grantor has the right to convey the ownership of the property.

3. Covenant Against Encumbrances: A promise by the Grantor, that the property is not encumbered, and is indeed able to be conveyed.

4. Covenant to Warrant and Forever Defend

Title: A promise by the Grantor, to make right any issues that might arise in the future in regards to the title, in benefit of the Grantee.

You might be thinking right now, my dear reader, "My head is spinning! I'll never understand this stuff!!" That is really to be expected, especially if you've never even heard someone trying to explain these terms, and even more so if up until now, you've never dealt with deeds, or have always assumed the lawyers will take care of everything. As this author mentioned before, a good real estate lawyer will be able to write up these deeds and make sure the transactions go off without a hitch, however, understanding the basics will give you a leg up on the competition!

Here is a scenario to help you better

understand what is taking place behind the scenes. You own a property, you want to sell that property, and you use a General Warranty Deed to convey the title. All that has happened here is, you have promised the buyer that you do in fact own the property that is being sold, you have the right to sell property, there are no hidden liens that the buyer does not know about, and if some issues arises in the future with the title, you are simply promising the buyer that you will help sort the problem out so he can keep his property. It's really all common sense when you think about it right?

As this author mentioned before, there are many ways to customize these deeds. Even though there are standard warranties implied with General Warranty Deeds, there are perfectly legal exceptions to these rules. For example, you might not be the only owner of the property. There might be co-owners, including spouses, estates, companies etc. There might be liens on the property being conveyed, such as an old mortgage loan that was never settled, or even old tax debts. The Grantor might not want to warrant the state of the property, which might lead to an "as is"[9] clause to be included in the deed, essentially limiting the Grantees right to bind the Grantor if there is an unknown defect to the property. These are all perfectly legal clauses and very common place when you dig into the fine print. So, how do Special Warranty Deeds differ?

---

[9] Literally, the property comes as it sits.

Subsection 2

Special Warranty Deeds

Special Warranty Deeds are almost exactly like the General Warranty Deeds you learned about in the previous section. They still adhere to all the covenants and warranties that are implied and expressed, yet there is still a key difference to consider. Special Warranty Deeds only bind the Grantor to the Grantee for issues that arise during the time the Grantor owned the property. Special Warranty Deeds do not bind the Grantor for issues that arose before them.

What does that mean?

Let us return to the previous sections example, you have a house, and you sell that house to a new buyer without any issues arising during the transaction. Sometime later, a person arrives at the property, and challenges the current owner's right to title. After further investigation, it turns out that the person who originally sold you the property in question, was a sibling who didn't have the right to sell that property. Now, you've sold the property to a new buyer, and the sibling that was left out of the loop originally, wants his share of the profits!

Under the Covenant to Warrant and Forever Defend Title from a General Warranty Deed, you would be bound to defend the current owner and clear up this mess. However, the Special Warranty Deed only applies this covenant if the issue had arisen from a problem caused during your ownership. In the example above, that issue arises from an ownership dispute before your tenure, therefore you are not bound to help the Grantee. This is *the* key distinction to draw between General Warranty Deeds and Special Warranty Deeds.

You might be wondering now, dear reader, how this distinction differs from a General Warranty Deed with an "as is" clause? It differs greatly, because the "as is" clause only applies to the state of the property, not the state of the title. That is the entire point of this section, the only real difference between the two deeds is when the Grantor can be bound. Other than that, both deeds can still be modified, and clauses can be added or deleted as needed. It's important to remember that this does not make the Special Warranty Deed any less affective, it's just another form of deed that can be used. Although, you are not very likely to see a Special Warranty Deed in residential transactions, since they are almost

exclusively used only in commercial settings.

Subsection 3

Quitclaim Deeds

Quitclaim Deeds are often misunderstood, and there are very good reasons. First and foremost, depending on who you ask, Quitclaim Deeds are not actually deeds at all! The purpose of a deed is to serve as an instrument to convey equitable and legal title to a property. Quitclaim Deeds, however, are only stating that the Grantor "quits"[10], or ceases, to have any interest in the property. Here's the rub, the Grantor signing the Quitclaim Deed is claiming to cease any interest, but they might not have interest to begin with!!

That is only the beginning of the oxymoron for the quasi deed. Having a Grantor

---

[10] Literally, to stop.

sign a Quitclaim Deed does not convey title to you, my dear reader, you still have to claim the title before you can possess the property in question, or risk being a squatter! This is usually accomplished with Adverse Possession, but there are still inherent risks associated with this style of conveyance. If a person with a valid claim arrives, they could evict you from the property you thought you owned, and you would have no recourse against the Grantor, because Quitclaims don't have any warranties whatsoever.

To make matters more convoluted, Title Companies will often not deal with properties being conveyed with Quitclaims, they will still require a more standard deed type. Luckily for you, my dear reader, there is always the option of a Deed Without Warranties. As you might have imagined from the name, this is a standard deed, only without any warranties implied or expressed. It is a much better option than Quitclaims, at least these are actual deeds that convey title, and they are better for the Chain of Title.

As you might remember, this Author stated that deeds are extremely capable of being modified to benefit either party, and Quitclaim Deeds versus Deeds Without Warranties are a perfect example of this concept. Quitclaims are extremely geared toward the Grantor, even going so far as to allow the possibility for the Grantor to have no real interest in the property being conveyed, in fact they do not even convey property to begin with. Deeds Without Warranties, at bare minimum, do bind the Grantor to having interest in the property, and convey that interest, even if there are no warranties to protect the Grantee later on.

At the end of the day, real estate investing is still a business. Every little opportunity to gain an edge will be exploited. That is why you must always be vigilant and knowledgeable, to protect yourself from potential downfalls.

Section 2

Real Estate Attorneys

For those of you reading this book, you might have noticed there is a number of references to taking legal matters to Real Estate Attorneys. There is an excellent reason for this, in all of the occasions this Author has needed a lawyer, it has been an investment that has paid off time, and time again! Does that mean you should always hire an Attorney? Do you specifically need a Real Estate Attorney, or will any Attorney suffice? These are all excellent questions, which is why this Author has consulted with an expert for this specific chapter.

The expert that was consulted is Attorney John Mitchell who currently resides in Texas.

Attorney Mitchell has made assurances, dear readers, that while this information is specific to Texas, it's still very universal across the fifty states. Of course, if you should have any questions about the information in this section, always consult an Attorney in your area. This chapter is not intended in aiding to find an Attorney, but simply in explaining the differences between a Real Estate Attorney, and a general Attorney.

In the state of Texas, all legal specializations are handled by the Texas Board of Legal Specialization. There are twenty-one categories that an Attorney can specialize in, and Real Estate is one of those categories, which is further broken down into three subsets; residential, commercial, and rural land. It is estimated that there are roughly seventy-thousand Attorneys practicing in Texas alone, however, only seven-thousand have a specialization.

The process to become specialized is quite demanding, as an Attorney can only apply to become specialized after five years of practice, and three years in the field they are seeking specialization in. Even after the time considerations, an Attorney seeking specialization in Real Estate, must also pass an exam designed to test that Attorney's overall knowledge in their field, as well as all the specific documentation they might have to draft, and even the special procedures they might have to adhere to! Once all of these requirements have been met, then an Attorney certified by the Texas Board of Legal Specialization can officially advertise himself as a specialist.

After a quick glance at all of the requirements, it is easy to deduce that a specialist will incur a much higher fee than a general Attorney. However, a specialist will, in theory, also deliver a much higher quality of work. So, which one should you choose? Unfortunately, there is no "one size fits all" answer to this question. For this Author, the deciding factor has usually been the people skills of the Attorney. How does the Attorney treat you? Do you feel as if the Attorney takes great pains in explaining the issues, and making sure you understand? Everybody has different requirements they look for.

Attorney John Mitchell had this to say about the matter. "If I were personally looking for an attorney to handle a real estate matter for me, I would first ask myself 'Can I afford to hire a specialist?' If the answer is 'no' then the rest of the analysis does not even matter. Assuming I can even afford an attorney specialist, then the question becomes, 'does my matter require such special knowledge to make it worth it?' In that case I would ask two more questions. First, 'How difficult and complex is my matter?' Second, I would ask 'how much time and money do I stand to lose if this should get messed up?' If my matter were simple and had pretty low stakes, then I would probably forgo the additional cost and just go to a general practitioner. If the matter is very complex and has a high likelihood of getting screwed up... and especially, if there is a lot of money on the line, I would try and go with a specialist."

If you are feeling a little overwhelmed, then there is good news for you. There is one saving grace, one rule that will protect the uninformed. It is an ethical rule that an Attorney only take on cases that are not beyond their legal capabilities, or expertise! There you have it, dear readers, if you cannot decide if you require an expert, then simply go to a general Attorney, and know they will refer you if your case is too complicated.

Section 3

Title Companies

Title Companies are mostly known for providing Title Insurance, however, they are sort of a one stop shopping for closing real estate transactions. In addition to Title Insurance, Title Companies serve as a clearing house for deeds. In a traditional real estate deal, one might visit a Title Company when they are first interested in a property. Title Companies can do a preliminary check on the status of a title, and can provide more services up until the end of the process.

After the preliminary check, one can choose to use the Title Company as an escrow service, and make their earnest money deposit with them to begin the process of purchasing a property. When the lender is making their decision on originating a mortgage, they will rely heavily on the title research of the Title Company, which has access to databases that can track title ownership, and will help to rectify any issues in title before the process moves forward. For example, they might requests that certain individuals fill out Marriage Affidavits, or search out the possible living heirs to a title who might later come along, and cause issues to the current owners.

Even when the lender decides to originate a mortgage, it is standard practice for them to use the escrow services of the Title Company that the buyer started their journey with. Title Companies will issue Title Insurance to the lender, known as the "Mortgagee Policy", which protects the lender for the value of the property, or the value of the loan, the lesser of the two, and remains in place until the note matures. The buyer can also receive Title Insurance during the purchase, which protects the buyer against equity loss should title issues arise in the future, and the policy remains in place as long as the buyer has equity interest. Fun fact, it is customary for the lender to pay for the buyer's insurance policy, but it's not a requirement.

There is still one more service that most Title Companies provide, they also have a lawyer to write up the deeds that will be issued after closing. Just to recap, Title Companies will; do preliminary research, escrow services, rectify title issues, ensure all the proper paperwork gets signed, and provide a lawyer to write up the deeds. It's easy to see why Title Companies have dominated

the market in traditional real estate!

Section 4

Mortgages

When people imagine a scenario where a Mortgage is needed, they often envision a young couple about to embark on their first major purchase. This is not entirely without merit, as that is the most common use for Mortgages. That is not the only use, however, as Mortgages are common in real estate investing as well, and have plenty of use even in Creative Investing!

It's important to understand that, Mortgages have many variations, and can become quite complex. This Author is not writing a book about Mortgages, but rather Creative Investing. Since Mortgages do have a place in that world, then they will be covered, but this is only a superficial dive into the most basic form for a Mortgage.

The most common lender for a Mortgage is a bank. Banks write Mortgages for individuals that don't have enough money to outright buy a property. The bank will usually require that the individual provide certain paperwork, agree to a credit check, be able to provide a down payment, and earnest money to the seller of the property. The down payment amount can vary, but in investment transactions 20% of the total purchase price is standard. If all of these conditions are met, the bank will "originate"[11], or write the Mortgage, and loan the individual the money they need to purchase the property.

---

[11] Term associated with mortgage underwriting. To originate means, to create the mortgage.

The buyer doesn't usually receive the money that is being loaned, but rather, that money is sent into an "escrow account"[12], which might be managed by the Title Company handling the closing, or an Attorney. After the closing occurs, the buyer will receive a deed to the property purchased, as well as their new Mortgage, usually referred to as the "note", and the bank receives a deed of trust. The deed of trust allows them to foreclose on the buyer of the property, should they fail to provide their Mortgage payments.

Of course, this is an extreme oversimplification of the entire process, which might take months to finish. For example, while banks are the most common Mortgage lenders, there are also Mortgage

---

[12] Legal term, meant to apply to actual numbered accounts used to hold money on behalf of others.

Companies, which will originate and fund the Mortgage themselves. Private lenders can also accomplish this, either in venture with a Mortgage Company, or on their own, though usually with an Attorney overseeing the transaction.

Naturally, there is a splendid Creative Investing opportunity that presents itself when dealing with Mortgages. One, being the Wraparound Transaction, will be covered later on in this book, since that is a bit advanced for someone that is just beginning. For now, my dear reader, just imagine the possibilities of writing your own Mortgage for a new buyer, and better yet, selling that Mortgage for a quick profit!

You read that correctly, Mortgages can be, and often are, sold after being originated. You could, as a savvy Creative

Investor, purchase up a property dirt cheap,

then after a tiny cash investment for minor

repairs, sell that property with a Mortgage.

As soon as the ink is dry on the paperwork,

you can turn around, and sell that Mortgage

for a small percentage off the top. There are

plenty of companies that gladly buy good debt

like this, they normally have investors that

provide them with cash by buying securities,

and they simply manage the Mortgage until it

is paid off, or sold again!

That is just one way to leverage

Mortgages in your favor, and there are plenty

of other iterations that won't be covered

here. There is the Negative Amortization

Mortgage, wherein the loan amount actually

increases in size with each payment. The

Interest-only Lifetime Mortgage, which allows

payments on interest, and lasts for the lifetime of the borrower. This Author is partial to the concept of the Reverse Mortgage, normally these are reserved for older borrowers. The loan is made on the equity of their property, they receive monthly installments, and the loan is due when they sell, pass away, or move out of the home for a consecutive period of time. Unfortunately, or fortunately depending on your viewpoint, this is not a book on Mortgages.

Chapter 3
Marketing

Section 1

Supply

For the purposes of this book, real estate supply will refer to foreclosed properties. When imagining supply, it's best to conjure up an image of a pyramid. Properties owned by the banks would be at the top of the pyramid, followed closely by properties sold by servicing companies, mutual funds, and other companies, then you would have properties sold by investors, and at the bottom you would have properties sold by owners. The reason for a property being at the top of the pyramid, as opposed to the bottom, is directly proportional to its market price, with the top consisting of below market prices, and the bottom consisting of properties at, or above market value.

Volume is the primary culprit for the disparity in prices between the top, and the bottom of the pyramid. When dealing with owners at the bottom of the pyramid, it's easy to imagine them owning one property, maybe it's the same house they bought when they were young, and making their very fist property purchase. When the time comes to sell, they want to maximize the earnings on the property, which leads to prices comparable, or higher than market value.

As you move up the pyramid, you will come across investors that move multiple properties a year, and can afford to sell at lower prices. Moving up through the mutual funds, and servicing companies, properties become numbers on a spreadsheet containing hundreds, or even thousands at a time, which leads to regular sales, thus more earnings, and lower prices per property. Of course, at the very top you have banks, and other lending institutions, which contain tens of thousands of properties on their balance sheets, and since we're talking about houses obtained through foreclosures, these properties are almost certainly listed *well* below market value.

You might be wondering, dear reader, how do you tap into the supply at the top of the pyramid? That entirely depends on your networking skills, but even more so, on your perseverance. By far the best asset you contain is your willingness to not give in. Even if you feel like you're beginning to bother your suppliers, it's important to maintain constant pressure. The thought to keep in mind is this, these properties will be bought, and sold whether you're involved, or not. If you don't lift a single finger to make a contact, and put deals together, the market will still continue to go on!

Another thought to keep in mind is, you shouldn't attempt to source properties from the top of the pyramid, at least not at first. Banks are rigid institutions, that don't want to deal with new businesses, especially if you're only going to move a few properties at a time. Banks have servicing companies moving thousands of properties for them, unless you're at that level, it's no use trying to make a connection at the top.

Those servicing companies, though, are a solid target to shoot for! Servicing companies don't want to deal with small time, one off investors, but if you're able to make contact with someone at one of those companies, and at least move a few properties a month, they will most likely continue to answer your calls. As far as finding these companies goes, the easiest way is to simply do an online search, you'll be amazed how easy it is to find them. Simply type in "servicing companies", and you're off to the races!

Once you have a few interesting prospects, you have a couple of choices to make. Most people will simply pick up the phone, and start "cold calling"[13] these companies looking for properties. This is not a bad option, but it is terribly inefficient. The other option is to search these companies on social media sites, and try to find "Portfolio Managers", or "REO Managers" that

---

[13] Sales term, meant to signify a prospective lead that doesn't know you.

work for these companies. Once you find someone, simply contact them through the social media site, or even email. This will yield much higher results, since you're specifically targeting the people in charge of selling the foreclosed properties. Remember, perseverance is key, keep contacting these people until they respond, it might not be a pleasant response, but they deal with many new inquiries every day, you have to keep contacting them if you hope to cut through the noise!

Once you've been searching, and contacting prospects for a few weeks, you should have all the contacts you need to source properties. Even a couple of contacts can provide *thousands* of properties a month, which is probably more than you could feasibly move. Of course, once you have supply you need

to create demand, and theoretically, the sky
will be limit.

Section 2

Demand

Creating demand will probably be the easiest step in your business. It's pretty well understood that, if you have the deals, you can always find a buyer. Since you're sourcing your properties from near the top of the pyramid, you'll have plenty of houses at below market prices, which will *almost* sell themselves. You will also notice that, finding buyers will become less time intensive as your business grows, because a lot of buyers will come back for more after the first deal!

You don't have to be a marketing genius to find your buyers, there are plenty of proven methods that exist today. This Author does not care for some of the more traditional methods, such as placing "bandit signs"[14], or advertising in online classifieds. These methods are not always very sustainable, and worse, they are not easily scalable! Of course, to each their own, if you feel comfortable using these methods, and they yield results, by all means use what you know. You're in the business of making money, so this Author will not discourage you from using something that is working.

There are more efficient, and scalable, methods to choose from. One method that begins slowly, but ramps up significantly over time, is to simply begin building a list of potential buyers. There are plenty of sites that offer landing pages, on which you can write simple, straightforward copy to attract

---

[14] Signs placed illegally. Signs placed in places they are not allowed to be, or placed without permission.

potential buyers. People will gladly give you their name, email, and even a phone number, if you offer to help them buy cheap properties.

If you're enterprising, you can easily use an online advertising service, which will allow you to build, and budget ads that appear for buyers looking for your services. These ads are cheap, and fairly automated once they're in place. In as short a time as a couple of weeks, you could start to build a list of dozens of potential buyers.

To round off your campaign, you can enlist the services of a email provider. A lot of good websites let you sign up for a low monthly fee, and send automated emails to your growing list of buyers. You don't have to be an expert in writing copy either, sometimes the best approach is the simplest one, just write about the service you're offering, and wait for the offers to start rolling in!

This method will take an investment of time, and money, up front, but will bear fruit if you have perseverance. The more you advertise, the more buyers join your list, the more your list grows, the more people become interested, and contact you. It's a cycle that builds over time, once you begin making your first few deals, you'll also start growing a list of buyers that have dealt with you in the past, and will come back to deal with you in the future. After a while, you won't need to keep growing your list, you'll have more repeat business than you'll know what to do with.

If all of this seems too complicated, there's a simpler version you can implement.

Go to a social media site, build a single page for your business, with your contact information. Once that's in place, you can start advertising your business page, get people to follow your page, and simply post regular offers to drum up business. Most major social sites offer you the ability to do all of this in one place, so you don't even need to cobble together multiple services. No need to use a third party advertiser, build a list, or set up automated emails, if you get enough followers, the business will come rolling in on its own.

The most important lesson you can learn from this section is this, if you don't start, you won't succeed. You need to begin as soon as possible to grow your audience, because selling properties is a numbers game. It is simple mathematics, once you begin letting people know that you exist, and you offer what they want, you'll eventually start finding the right buyers. There's nothing wrong with hoping your fist contact will lead to your first sale, but realistically, it's more likely to be your one-thousandth contact! That is why the best advice this Author can give you is, begin today!!

Section 3

Hard-Money Lending

Hard-money lenders can be a great resource for creative real estate investors looking to break into the business, but might not have the funds to get their first few deals off the ground. It could also lead to a horse head in your bed one morning. Certainly worth a look at the options either way!

When dealing with hard-money lenders, it's important to realize they have no real stake in your success. They usually will not do any work to move a deal along, and they don't really want to take time out of their schedule to teach you about the business. Hard-money lenders want to put up cash for a high "ROI"[15] with little to no downside. These types of lenders look for deals that are almost guaranteed to make money, which can be a good indicator on any deals you're trying to put together, after all, if even a hard-money lender won't touch it, that deal might not be as good as you imagined. If they do agree to participate, they will insist on a high interest rate, equity participation, and possibly a personal guarantee.

You can't really do much about the high interest payments, but you should really make absolutely sure that a hard-money lender is your only option. Dig really deep, and be sure there isn't an old Aunt Betty who might loan you the money instead. If the deal is good enough to stand on its own, there is nothing wrong with keeping the earnings in the family. If there is no other option, then you simply

---

[15] An acronym which stands for Return On Investing.

have to contend with the interest.

There is still the issue of equity
participation, which is a cut out of the
earnings the property will make after closing.
You can, and should, deal with the question of
equity participation up front. There's nothing
wrong with negotiating a reasonable cap on the
percentage of equity, or simply trade the
equity participation for a flat payment,
either way, it's not advised to leave the cap
open ended. If dealt with properly, you should
be able to close your deal, repay the loan
with interest, write a check for the equity
participation, and still walk away with a
substantial gain. Otherwise, you're
structuring your deals wrong, or not choosing
high margin deals in the first place.

Even if you have to contend with high

interest, and maneuver an equity participation, there is absolutely no reason to sign a personal guarantee. If your hard-money lender insists on this, then run away as fast as you can! Hard-money lending should be based on the strength of the deal alone, don't be conned into thinking you also have to risk yourself to make the deal happen. This should be a red flag, either your deal is weak, or your lender is looking to take you for a ride. A golden rule this Author always suggests is, if you can't walk away from the deal without risking your business, it's not a deal you should be considering.

If you've made it this far into negotiations, then your lender should have no problems with you bringing in your lawyer to look over the paperwork. Your lawyer might, and should, suggest some parameters to protect you once the deal is signed. For example, it would be wise to include provisions for extending the loan, everything takes twice as long, and costs twice as much as expected. Your lawyer should tweak any "default provisions"[16] to allow time for defaults to be cured, and of course, due-on-sale provisions are a no-no with hard-money lending. You don't want a lender accelerating loans when you least expect it!

Keeping these thoughts in mind should help you navigate the shark infested waters, and keeping a good Attorney handy doesn't hurt. No offer is an "offer you can't refuse", so don't let a hard-money lender push you around. It's your deal, it's your business, but most importantly, it's your decision to

---

[16] Terms in a contract which determine what is to be done if the borrower is late, or unable to pay.

move forward.

Chapter 4

Deal Structures

Section 1

Flipping Contracts

For the majority of beginners in Creative Real Estate, the first type of deals they'll put together are contract flips. It's a simple deal that only requires a buyer, and a property they're interested in. If you've studiously learned from the last chapter, you should have no problem obtaining the two crucial parts to putting together this deal.

No matter which method you choose to find them, the first thing you need are buyers. Whether you choose to grow a list, or simply begin to grow a following, will slightly alter the way you can approach this issue. If you chose to grow a list, then you simply need to survey your potential buyers for what properties they're in need of. If a following is more your style, then you don't need to survey anyone, you can just pick good properties, and wait for offers to roll in.

Either one of the two options mentioned above is a solid choice, but for the purposes of flipping contracts, growing a following might be slightly more advantageous. This Author would suggest beginning with any number of followers that you have, but around one hundred is when the business starts to smooth out, and you can begin to see a pattern of buyers emerge. You can choose to survey them to find out what zip codes, and price ranges are desired, though that's not absolutely necessary. A good rule of thumb is to choose popular cities to source your properties from, a quick internet search will steer you in the right direction if needed, and try to choose properties between one-hundred to one-hundred and fifty thousand dollars market value.

The reason for the price cap is, if you take twenty to forty percent off the top, you can potentially end up with properties ranging from sixty to ninety thousand, which is the sweet spot for average investors. You'll see a much higher turnover of properties at this price range, and flipping contracts does generate smaller margins, so speed is key here. The speed required for this method is why having a following of potential buyers works so well.

You'll be receiving property listings from your suppliers on a regular basis, probably during the beginning of each month, and there will probably be a deadline for turning in offers. You can ask your supplier for these dates, as well as what discounts are more likely to be accepted, twenty percent, thirty percent, thirty-five percent etc. You should also ask your supplier what fees are charged for each property sold, and factor that into the discounts.

If you know a property has a market value of one-hundred thousand, and your supplier will accept as low as sixty-five thousand to close, plus a three thousand dollar fee, then you can offer that property for seventy-three thousand dollars. That accounts for the discounted rate, minus the supplier's three-thousand dollar fee, and nets you a hefty five-thousand in the process. Study that calculation until you can recite it in your sleep, because this is your formula for pricing properties.

So now you have to follow a simple routine. You'll receive your spreadsheets during the first of the month, with a deadline probably two to three weeks later. Every morning choose a few properties, adjust their pricing like above, and blast those offers to your followers. You can provide an email for them to contact you, or a phone number, even if it rings straight to a voicemail. Every morning simply choose new properties, and wait for the offers to come in every afternoon. When interested buyers contact you, as for their contact information, and tell them they have three to five days to do their due diligence. Experienced buyers should have no problems with this deadline, and should submit offers quickly.

Your supplier will most likely require a deposit, probably twenty percent of the total, so you'll need to specify to your buyer that a deposit is necessary when submitting an offer. The deposit amount that you give your buyer, should include the amount required by your supplier, plus their fee, and your fee as well. When the buyer submits their offer, plus their deposit, you forward an offer to your supplier, minus your fee. If the supplier accepts the offer, you now have the property "under contract"[17], and the supplier will send you a contract made out to you "or your assigns"[18]. This part is extremely important, the contract has to include assigns. This way, you can simply sign the contract over to your buyer, and walk away with your fee. Now you know how to flip contracts!

---

[17] Real estate term, having a property under contract means you have the exclusive option to purchase for a time period.

[18] Real estate term, an assign is a person who has been given the rights, and responsibilities of a contract.

Section 2

Flipping Houses

Learning how to flip contracts has really laid the foundation for this section. Flipping houses is almost exactly like flipping a contract. There is more legwork involved, but there is a also a much larger margin for profit as well! So what differences can you expect?

The first noticeable difference will be in the style you choose to grow your list of buyers. With contract flipping having a following was a good strategy for quickly closing deals, but with house flipping you need a more involved approach. Since you're going after bigger profit margins, you need to do some of the work ahead of time. You need to get to know your buyer on a deeper level, what property type they're after, price range, zip codes, and condition of the property. You have to do a bit of due diligence even before your buyer receives a listing from you.

The biggest advantage to flipping houses, is that you also get to keep your supplier a trade secret. In contract flipping, you simply sign the contract over, and it's up to the buyer to follow up with your supplier, and close that pending deal. You'll be more involved with house flipping, but you'll also provide a higher level of service, earn more profit, and maintain your supplier for yourself.

So you'll be doing more work to grow your list of buyers up front. It would be wise to send a questionnaire to anyone that wants to be on your list, and find out all of their preferences as soon as they join. You should also explain from the beginning that each buyer needs to be able to produce "proof of funds"[19] before submitting any offers, and that there will be a deposit, which you will calculate to include the fee that your supplier charges. You can choose to let buyers know that you will charge a fee, anywhere from ten-thousand to fifteen-thousand, or not, it's okay either way. This Author would also advise to require a signed Non-Disclosure Agreement when a buyer joins your list, since it will further protect your business, but this is entirely optional as well.

Now the routine that you follow for houses, is very similar to the routine you

---

[19] Real estate term, proof of funds may simply be a bank statement that shows a balance sufficient to cover expenses.

followed for contracts. When your supplier provides you with property listings, you pick the properties that best suit each of your buyers, and allow them time to do their due diligence. However, this time you've already done some of the due diligence yourself, because you're choosing properties *specifically* for those buyers. Now here is where the routine changes a little bit, you will definitely need to bring in an Attorney to finish these deals.

Your Attorney doesn't need to be an expert in real estate, but he should have an idea of what he's doing. When your buyer submits an offer with their deposit, they will be sending it to your Attorney's escrow account, or whoever is handling escrow services. Now you provide an offer to the supplier, and if they accept, the buyer will also be sending the rest of the money due to your Attorney's escrow, who will now perform a "double close"[20].

This entails that your Attorney research the title of the property first, and write up the warranty deed that will be issued to the buyer. After everything is registered in the proper real property records, your Attorney will forward the rest of the payment due for the sale to the supplier, and the deed to the buyer. Your Attorney will then subtract his fees, and the closing fees from the amount remaining, after which, he will forward the rest to you. As mentioned before, you should net a tidy ten to fifteen thousand dollars for this transaction, and if done correctly, should only take one to two weeks to complete.

---

[20] Real estate term, a double close literally means two closings, one right after the other.

As you can see, it's certainly more involved that simply flipping contracts, but the rewards can be much bigger, especially since you have *super* qualified buyers that have been vetted, and most likely will keep returning for more deals in the future.

Section 3

Wraparound Transactions

In the world of seller-financing, the wraparound transaction is a unique way for an investor to sell a property still under mortgage. In a standard wraparound, there are four parties involved to some degree, and at least four documents; a warranty deed, a wraparound deed of trust, a wrap note, and a wraparound agreement. It all begins after an enterprising investor purchases a property using a Mortgage.

The investor seeks out a buyer who agrees to the wraparound transaction. An Attorney will draft a wrap note for the sale of the property to the new buyer, complete with a wraparound agreement that outlines details such as, casualty insurance, when the payments are due, title insurance etc. It's important to note that, there should be casualty insurance in place for both the investor, and the new buyer. It's a little funky, but when dealing with wrapped notes, you never know what the insurance companies might say to wiggle out of paying a policy.

After the two parties execute the wrap note, the investor receives a wraparound deed of trust, securing the property, and allowing him to initiate a foreclosure should the new buyer default. The new buyer receives a warranty deed to the property, and a new Mortgage. In case you were wondering, dear reader, there is a *slight* possibility that this transaction will cause a "due-on-sale"[21] clause to kick in, however, that is extremely

---

[21] A provision included in the terms of a mortgage that allow a loan to be accelerated if the property securing that loan is no longer owned by the borrower.

rare. Technically speaking, it's perfectly okay for the owner of the lien on a property, and the owner of said property, to be two different people.

It should also be noted that, wraparound transactions are not the same as an "assumption"[22], in that the new buyer *does not* agree to take on the original debt owed to the lender. There are technically two liens in place, the original lien between the lender, and the investor, as well as a second lien between the investor, and the new buyer. The first lien is considered to be "wrapped" by the second lien, or the "junior loan"[23].

---

[22] An assumption is when a third party assumes the responsibility of paying a loan.

[23] If there are two loans using the same asset as security, and borrower defaults, the asset is sold, and the proceeds are used to pay the loans off in order. The junior loan would be second.

Of course, this is all just a basic example of a wraparound transaction, there can be more convoluted iterations. For example, the investor might have multiple Mortgages on the same property, which is still perfectly viable for a wraparound. It's also possible for the new buyer to secure his purchase, not with a standard Mortgage, but with a property of his own! This is for very advanced investors, so be sure to finish this book before attempting anything so difficult.

Chapter 5

Business Structures

Section 1

Business Structures

Structuring your business is an important issue to consider on your journey to creative investing mastery. While you need to ponder on tax implications, legal issues that might arise, as well as estate planning for the future, the *most* important issue to consider at first is how to get your first deal closed. You should not get bogged down on questions like these when you're just beginning, but if you're this far along the book, there's no reason to suspect you won't be asking these questions soon enough. It doesn't hurt to dip your toes in the water, right?

There are a lot of business entities to consider, however, since this book could not possibly cover all of the options, only a few

will be considered. Mainly, the Limited
Liability Companies, with a touch on their new
Series options, as well as Limited
Partnerships. There will also be a brief
subsection on trusts, for those of you
interested in estates.

All of these business entities are very common
in the world of real estate investing. They
are not, of course, an extensive study on the
subject, so you should consider consulting an
Attorney if you have any more questions. The
last section will outline some business models
that use these entities to the fullest, as
well as the information that has been covered
up to this point. Everything will be brought
together soon enough!

Subsection 1

Limited Liability Companies

If you're looking for a business entity that fits hand in glove with the real estate investment model, that would be the L.L.C. It is very easy to set up, flexible enough to change on the fly, and robust enough to scale as needed. Especially now that the Series L.L.C. is available! First thing's first, though, what is a limited liability company, and why do you need one?

Limited Liability Companies are a hybrid of a few business entities cobbled together, mostly Corporations, and Limited Partnerships. L.L.C.s take the benefits from the entities they're modeled after, and combine them all into one pretty useful set up. They're most popular feature, which also happens to be part of their namesake, is the idea of "Limited Liability"[24].

Limited Liability helps to protect the owners, or "Members", of the L.L.C. by limiting the financial liability to the fixed amount conversely related to the ownership percentage of each member. This is especially useful if the company is sued. For example, if a customer suffers some sort of injury from a product produced by an L.L.C., they'd have to sue the company, not the owners. If the customer were to win that lawsuit, then the damages would be paid in relation to how much ownership each member has in the company, essentially spreading out the risk.

---

[24] Limited Liability is the concept that one is not personally liable. In this instance, a member of an LLC cannot be personally liable to debtors of the LLC.

L.L.C.s also protect member's personal finances with their limited liability. If for some reason the company goes bankrupt, debtors have to recover from the L.L.C. Inversely, if a member is sued, or goes bankrupt, the L.L.C. is protected as well. Debtors coming after members would have to win a "charging order", which would protect the assets of the company by limiting how much debtors collect, and not giving a debtor any sort of rights to vote, or manage the company.

There is also a powerful tax advantage that can be gained from this business entity. By default, income earned by an L.L.C. will be reported on each member's personal income tax returns, and taxed at their rate. This helps to avoid the "double tax"[25] scenario that a

---

[25] The concept that a dollar earned will be taxed multiple times.

lot of Corporations suffer from, wherein income is taxed at the corporate level, then again when dividends are paid out to investors.

Perhaps the biggest draw to the L.L.C. model is how simple they are to maintain. In most jurisdictions L.L.C.s are not required to follow the same rigid regulations for maintaining documents that corporations, and other companies, have to follow. L.L.C.s are usually entitled to allow members to vote on how they will be managed, and thus allowing members to limit how much paperwork needs to be filed. This can be handy if the L.L.C. happens to have a small number of members, or even just one member, which is also perfectly fine.

For some select states there is also an

alternate version of the L.L.C. described

above, known as the Series L.L.C. This entity

allows the company to register "D.B.A.s"[26]

under its name, each one known as a Series of

that company, which act as their own entity

separate from the original L.L.C. For example,

you could have Original Series L.L.C., which

would register the D.B.A. as Original Series

L.L.C. D.B.A. Series A. Original Series L.L.C.

D.B.A. Series A, would act independently of

Original Series L.L.C., and could sue, or be

sued, without entangling the assets of the

parent company, or any other series under this

structure!

Each series could also maintain its own

financial records, and even have its own

managers. Meanwhile, for the purposes of

---

[26] An acronym which stands for Doing Business As.
Sometimes referred to as Assumed Names or Fictitious Names.

filing taxes, and other documentation, all could be channeled back up through the parent company for simplicity. It is a more versatile structure than even a standard L.L.C., and can surely be advantageous to an investor who might have multiple properties he wants to protect, but doesn't want to file for a new company each time. Just to be safe, forming a Series L.L.C., if it is indeed available in your jurisdiction, should *absolutely* be left to an Attorney with experience, it's not a job that can be accomplished on a website.

Subsection 2

Limited Partnerships

A Limited Partnership is an excellent business entity for the entrepreneur who wants to source investments for his enterprise, but does not want to share in the decision making. This structure acts similar to that of a corporation with shareholders, in that the shareholders receive "dividends"[27] payed out to them proportional to their investment in the company, but have to right to manage the day to day business. Limited Partnerships can be more restrictive with its investors than a corporation, at least in a corporation shareholders have some opportunities to vote on decisions, but in an L.P. that might not be the case depending on how it operates.

---

[27] Payments that are distributed to investors.

An L.P. usually has at least one "General Partner", as well as one "Limited Partner". The general partner carries all of the responsibility for the day to day running of the partnership, and does not enjoy the protection of limited liability. The limited partner does get limited liability privileges, but usually has no say in how the partnership is managed. In fact, unless otherwise stated, the general partner is the only one with authority to engage the partnership in business with a third party, or bind the partnership to a third party debtor.

An L.P. can have more than one general partner as well, and as many limited partners as it needs for raising capital. Being a limited partner is not necessarily a lifelong endeavor either, it's possible for limited partners to have a term partnership that expires after a certain time, or after they've recovered their original investment plus interest. It really all depends on how the partnership agreement is drafted, and how the partnership is run. It's important to note that the limited liability that the limited partner enjoys, also protects the partnership from any debtors that might try coming after the company. L.P.s are covered by the same laws that L.L.C.s are, and a debtor can only really hope to receive a charging order for the interest of a limited partner, and gains no rights to vote, or manage the company.

You might be wondering why a limited partner would be comfortable with handing over a large sum of money to invest in a company they can't manage. That's an excellent question my dear reader, a lot of advanced investors are looking for a good return, and want to invest in a good enterprise, but don't have the skills, or the desire to manage a company. In a later section you'll discover a good use for an L.P. that takes full advantage of this principle.

Subsection 3

Trusts

It's a shame this book is not a detailed guide on trusts, they are a very interesting subject to cover, and can be a powerful tool for any investor who wants to leave his assets behind for generations to come. This Author will try to highlight the tenets of a trust in broad strokes. In a style similar to that of the section on deeds, first there will be a series of points that explain some basics about trusts, then there will be some detailed examples to better narrow down the possible uses for a trust.

1. A trust is a document that can be drafted, and executed in private. An Attorney would have no problem drafting up a trust

document based on their client's needs.

2. A trust has three main parties involved; the trustor, who conveys the assets into the trust, the trustee, who manages the trust, and the beneficiary, who will benefit from the trust. All of these roles could be fulfilled by one person, or many, and could even be fulfilled by companies, or other trusts.

3. A trust can have a single asset, or multiple assets. These assets can be anything from real property, such as a house, to intangible property, such as a trademark.

4. There can be successor trustees, and successor beneficiaries, who don't have to be alive when the trust is formed.

5. Trusts can be; temporary, permanent, revocable, irrevocable, created while the trustor is alive, created after the trustor is deceased using a will, or created from a court order.

6. A trust is an excellent instrument for asset protection. A trust is considered to be "bankruptcy remote"[28], meaning that a creditor seeking to attain assets in a trust would have to go through extraordinary measures, and would probably require a court order to accomplish this.

There is a lot more minutia that could be explained, but for the purposes of this book these six points are sufficient to have a

---

[28] The concept that an asset is removed from bankruptcy proceedings. For example, if you declare bankruptcy, and the courts allow you to keep your home, your home is bankruptcy remote, and can not be claimed by debtors.

basic understanding. The most obvious benefit to a real estate investor is asset protection. Many investors hire Attorneys to draft up trust documents, then convey properties that are income generating into these trusts. It's possible for the investor to choose who will be the trustee, as well as the beneficiary, and all of those positions can be the investor.

It's also very common for an investor to set up a trust while alive, for the purpose of leaving their assets to their heirs, and bypassing the probate process. This method is much cleaner than a will, the assets will already be in place, and the beneficiary will begin benefiting whenever the right conditions are met. This could be when the beneficiary reaches a certain age, when the trustor passes away, or even a when a certain date is reached. It's also possible for the trustee to have full discretion, and only disburse the benefits to the beneficiary when they deem it proper.

The last example that will be explored is, using a trust as a form of seller financing. If you refer to the points made above, specifically point two, and point five, you will see how this can be accomplished. Since a trust can be temporary, it's possible for an investor to convey a property into a trust which is written to last until the property is completely paid for. Since it's also possible for a trust to have multiple beneficiaries, and for those beneficiaries to be practically anybody, it's possible to grant a percentage of benefit to the investor who will sell the property, and a percentage of benefit to the buyer. Once the buyer fulfills the requirements to buy the property, they simply attain the percentage of benefit owned by the investor, and become full owners of the trust themselves, at which point they can dissolve the trust, and attain the deed to the property.

This is a very advanced, and highly complicated procedure not to be undertaken by a novice. It would be extremely wise to involve an Attorney in the entire process, just to be sure no laws are accidentally broken. The main reason an investor might go through all of this trouble has to do with the fact that benefit ownership in a trust is considered personal property. Personal property doesn't necessarily fall into the executory contract provisions that real property does. These provisions can make owner financing a potential mine field, which is why one would be wise to involve a professional.

Section 2

Three Models

You've come a long way, my dear reader, since the beginning of this book. Along the way you've covered everything from real estate basics, to marketing, structuring deals, and now how to bring all of that knowledge together into an empire. Down below we'll cover three solid business models that use the information you've learned so far to build scalable businesses. All of the information you need to get started today has been provided, and if you have any questions you can reference back to the previous chapters to refresh your memory.

The first model is what this Author likes to refer to as the Concierge. It's a simple business structure that consists of building

up a list of potential clients, as well as a

list of suppliers. You should remember how to

accomplish this from Chapter 3. All you need

is to find the supply, the demand, and simply

begin to create deals between the two. You

simply cash in each time a deal closes, and

you repeat the process as many times as you

want. The more deals you close, the more you

can potentially close in the future, since a

lot of buyers will keep coming back for more.

If you want to add a little

sophistication to your business, you can move

up to the next model known as the

Entrepreneur. You'll need a dedicated

marketing budget at this point, and some

C.R.M. software would also be useful. At this

level of your business, you really want to

focus on making multiple connections with

frequent buyers, this will be the key to success. The best way to scale in the creative real estate market is to constantly have repeat business. This means you will need to invest quite a bit in increasing the number of new clients you get, and making sure you keep the clients you already have.

The most advanced business model that will be covered is the Mogul. At this point in your business, dealing with buyers, and suppliers, is no longer your main focus. You should have a strong business with regular weekly sales, and a workforce of employees to manage that business every day. What you should be focusing on now is finding investors, and building up a portfolio of rental properties, and owner financed properties. If you'll recall back to subsection 2 of this chapter, you already know what business entity will help with managing investors. Subsection 1, which deals with L.L.C.s will become more important now, especially if you live in state that allows Series L.L.C.s.

You'll need a regular L.L.C. to manage the general partnership of your L.P., as well as any business dealings that need to be done. A Series L.L.C., if it's available to you, will do nicely for holding all of those rental properties. The owner financed properties, which are really financed by the limited partners, can be sold, and the money can be reinvested into more rentals, after paying off the limited partners, and providing a nice ROI for them of course. All of proceeds from the rentals can be funneled into trusts, which will protect the money for generations to come.

Hopefully these models will give you some ideas of the possibilities that are available to you. It's been a long journey, but you made it until the end. You have now learned more about creative real estate, than most real estate investors. It is this Authors hope that all of the information that's been provided, will help to give you that edge that you need to succeed. Keep learning, my dear reader, and don't be afraid to try new ideas!

The End